I0409739

Color With Me!

Auntie & Me

The Christmas Shop

Coloring Book

Sandy Mahony
Mary Lou Brown

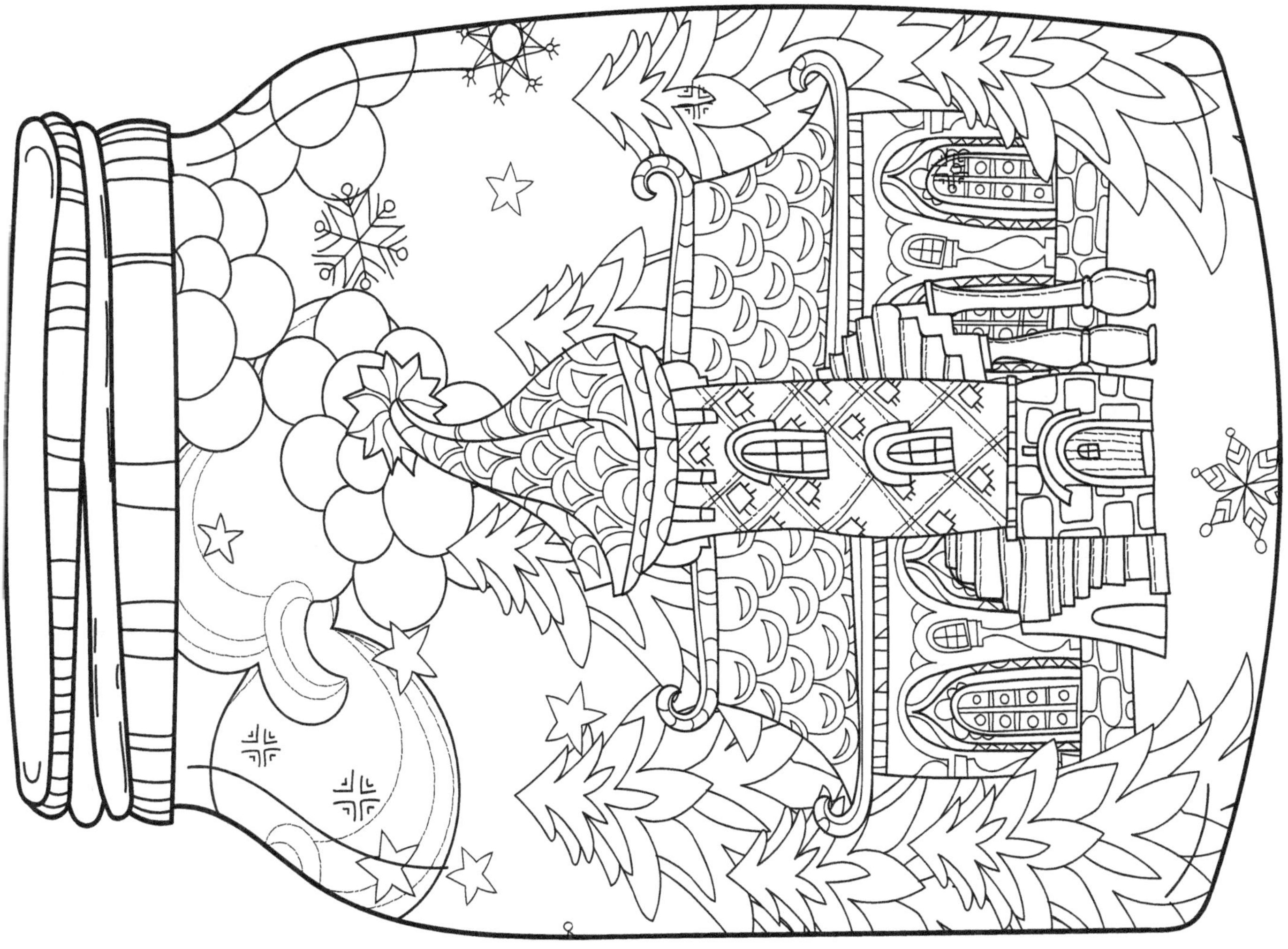

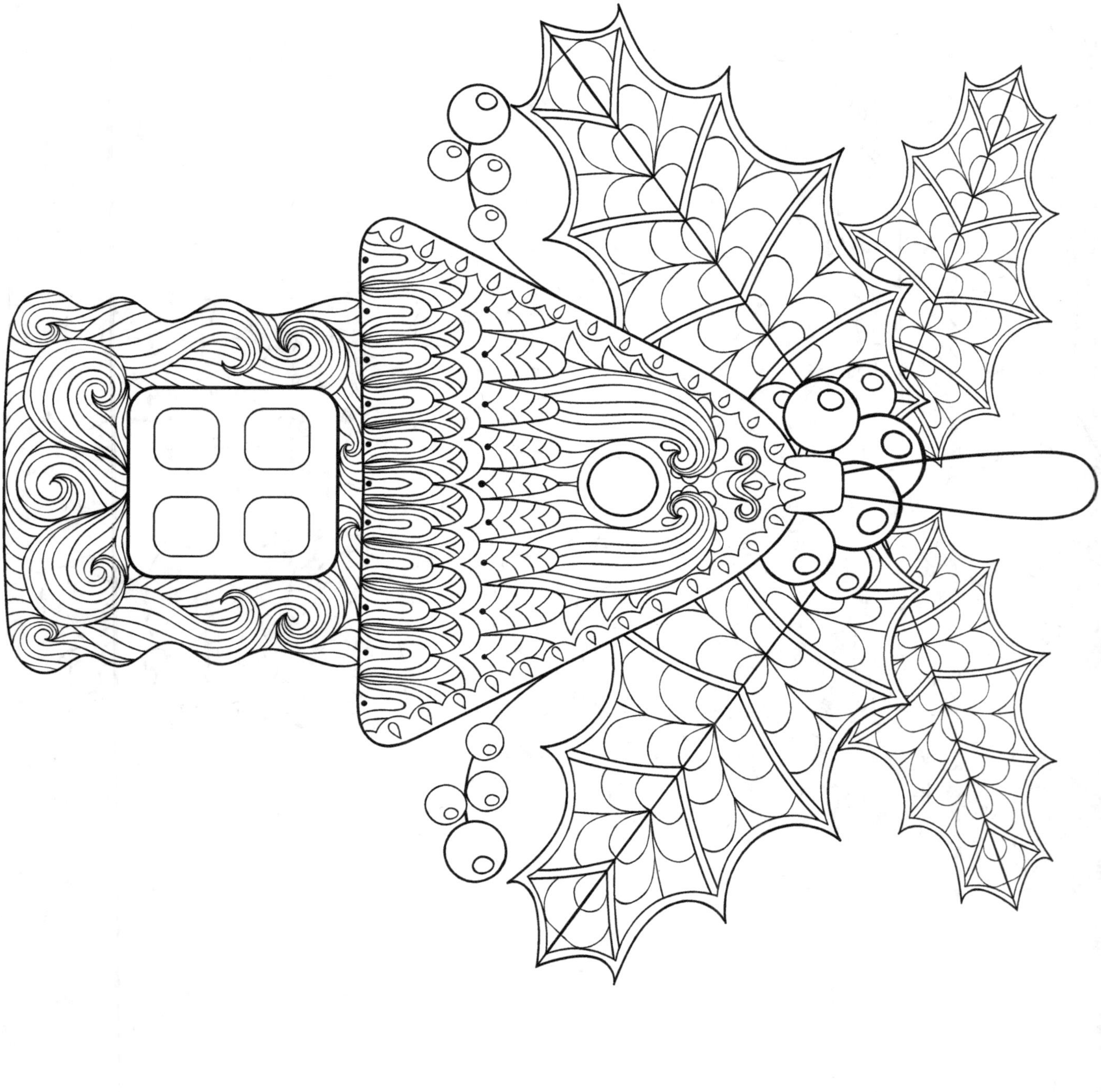

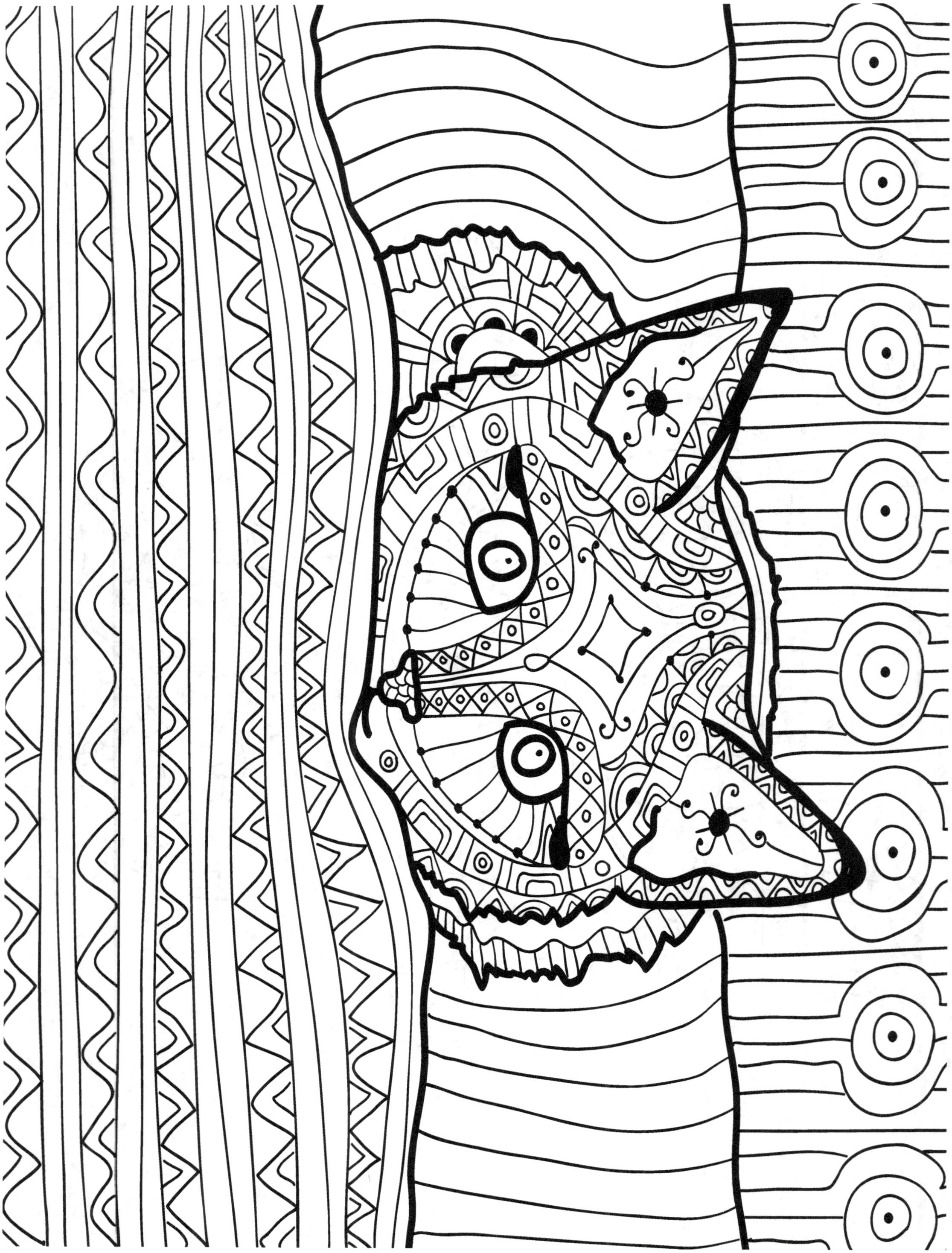

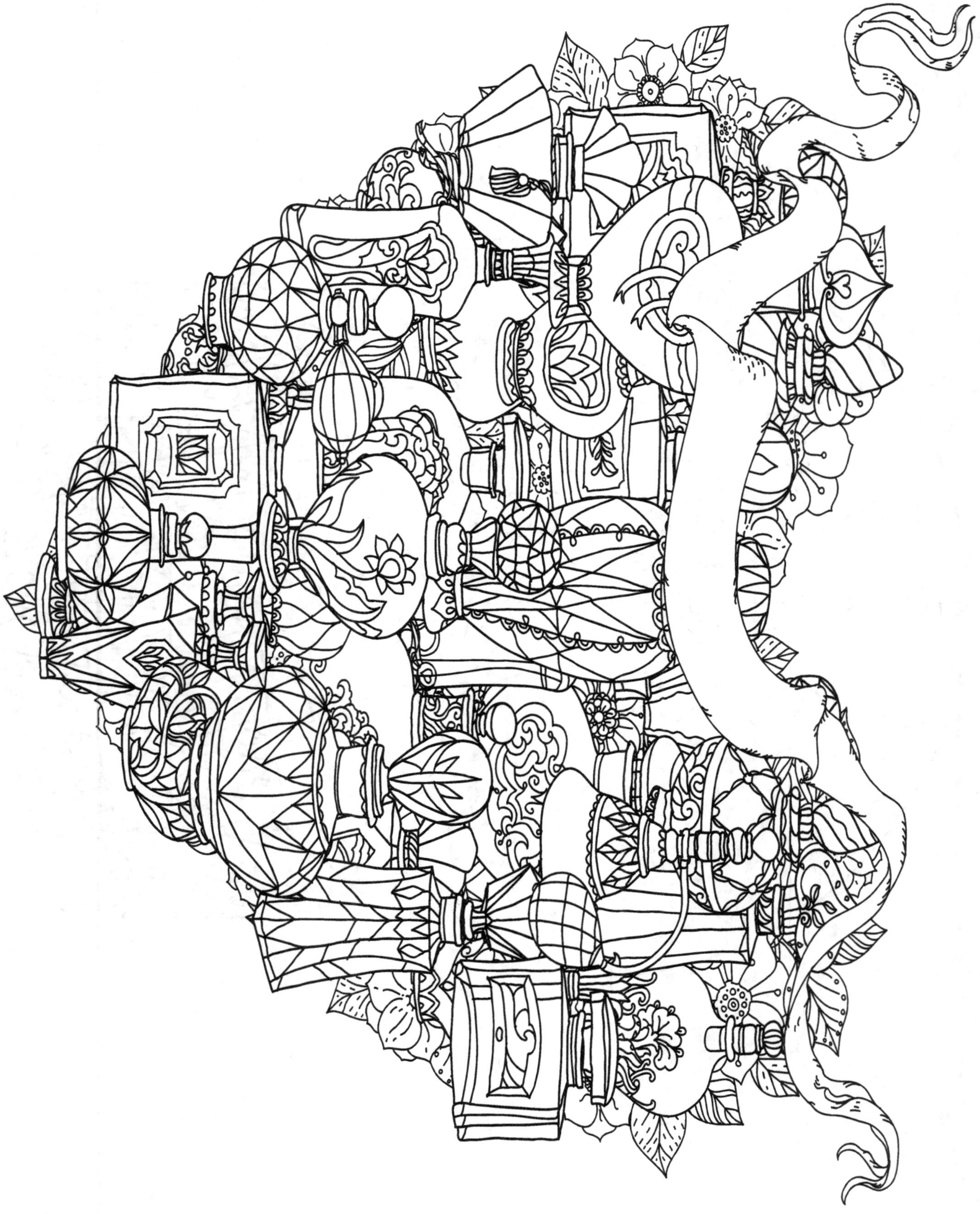

PERFUME

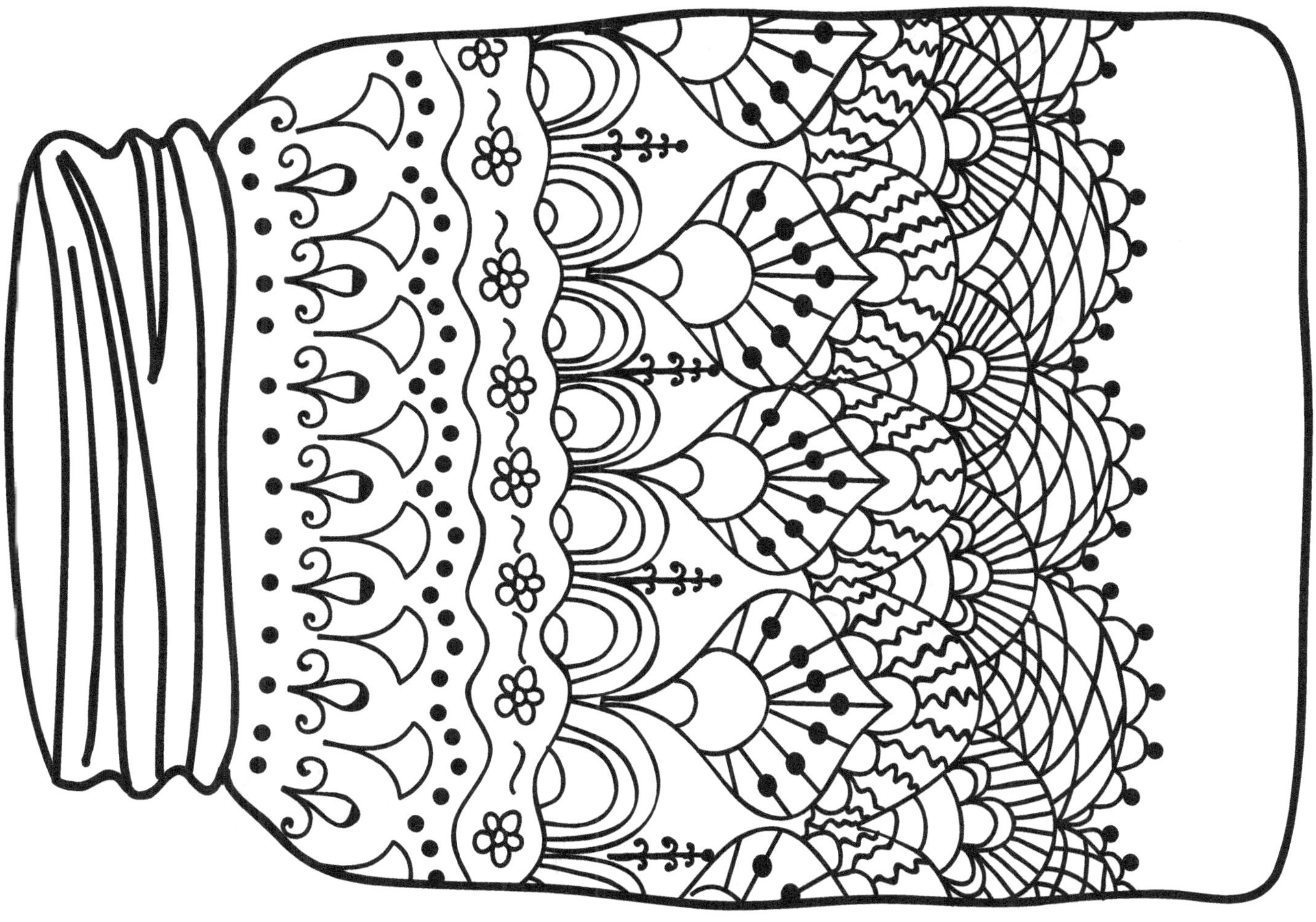

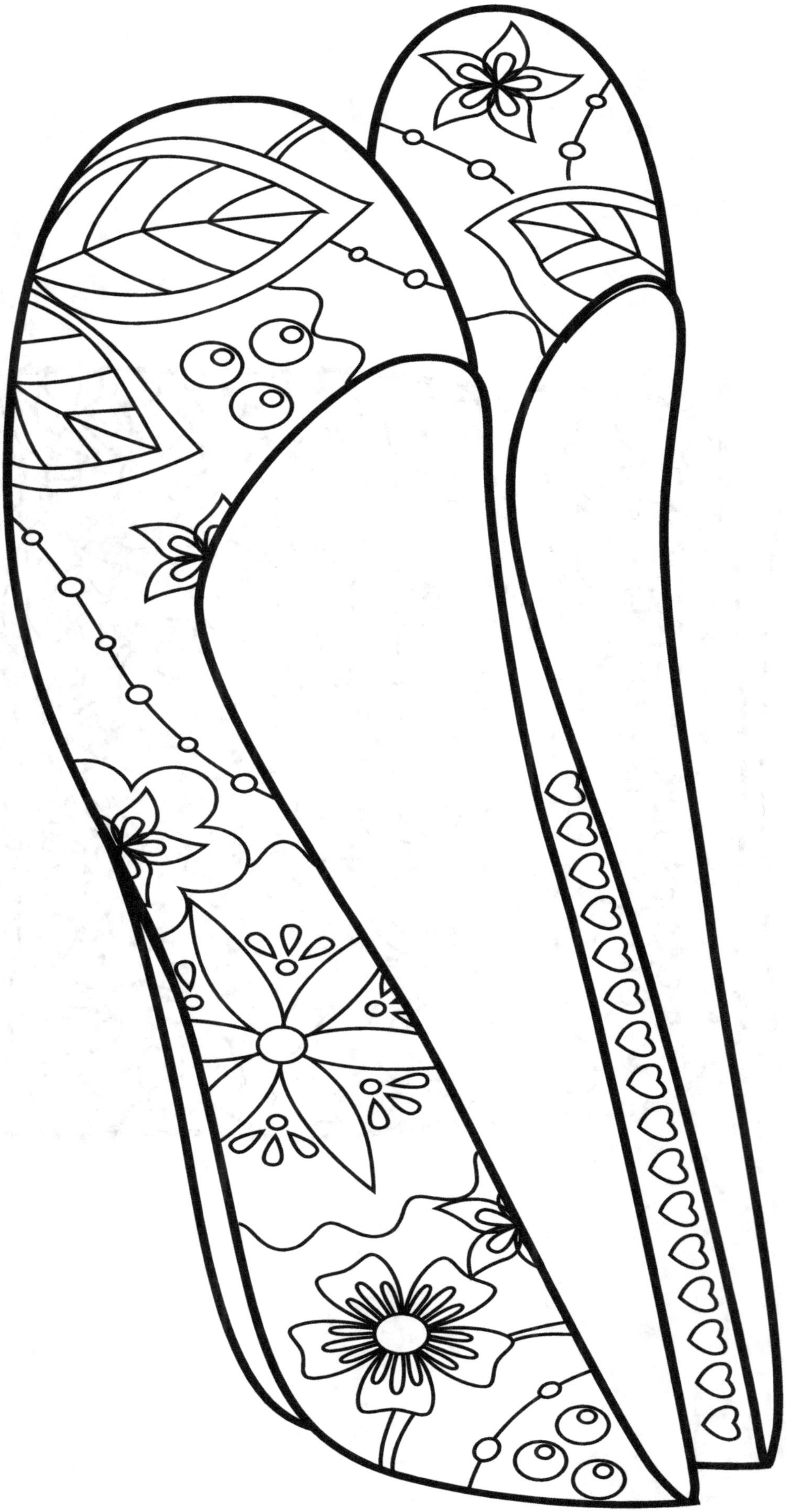

Merry
Christmas
Happy
New
Year!

Merry Christmas!

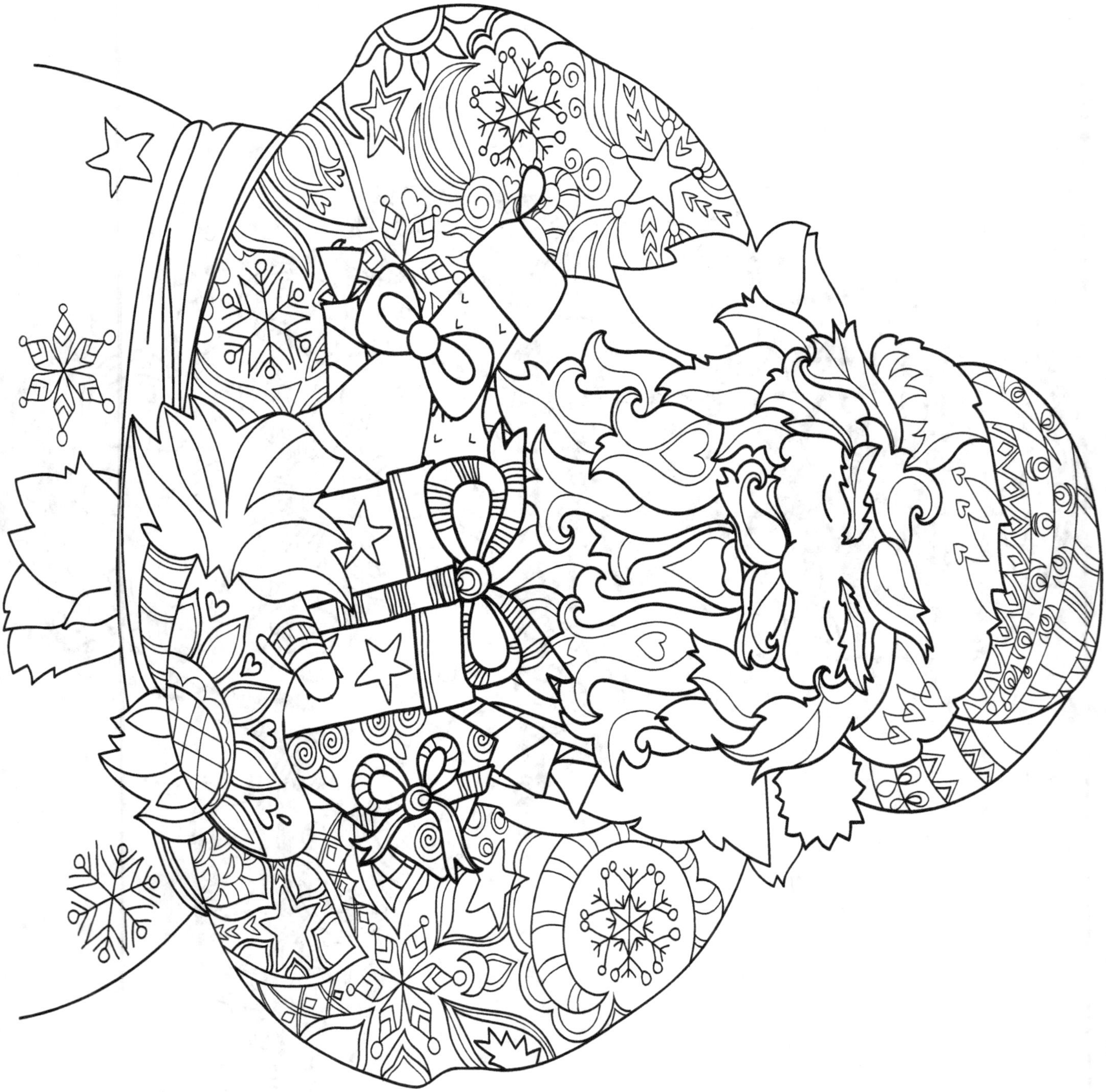

Merry
Christmas

Christmas

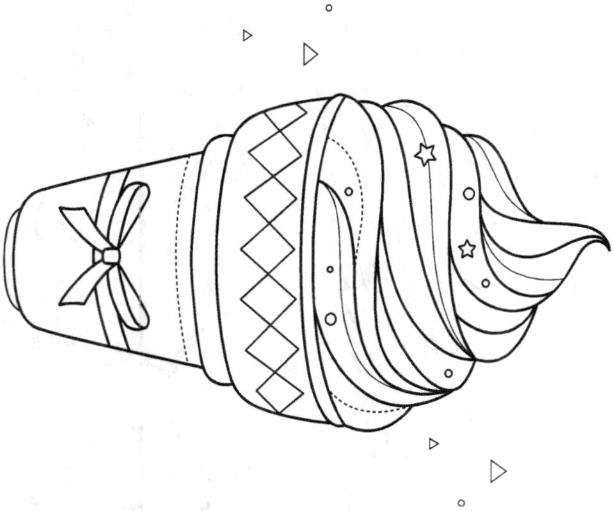

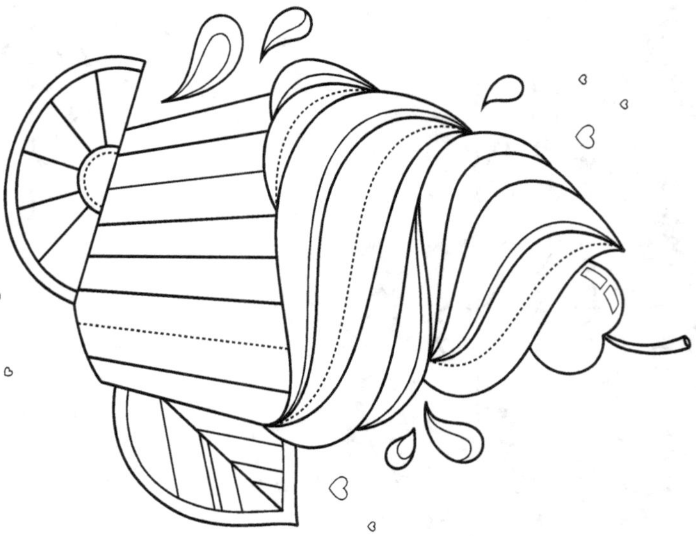

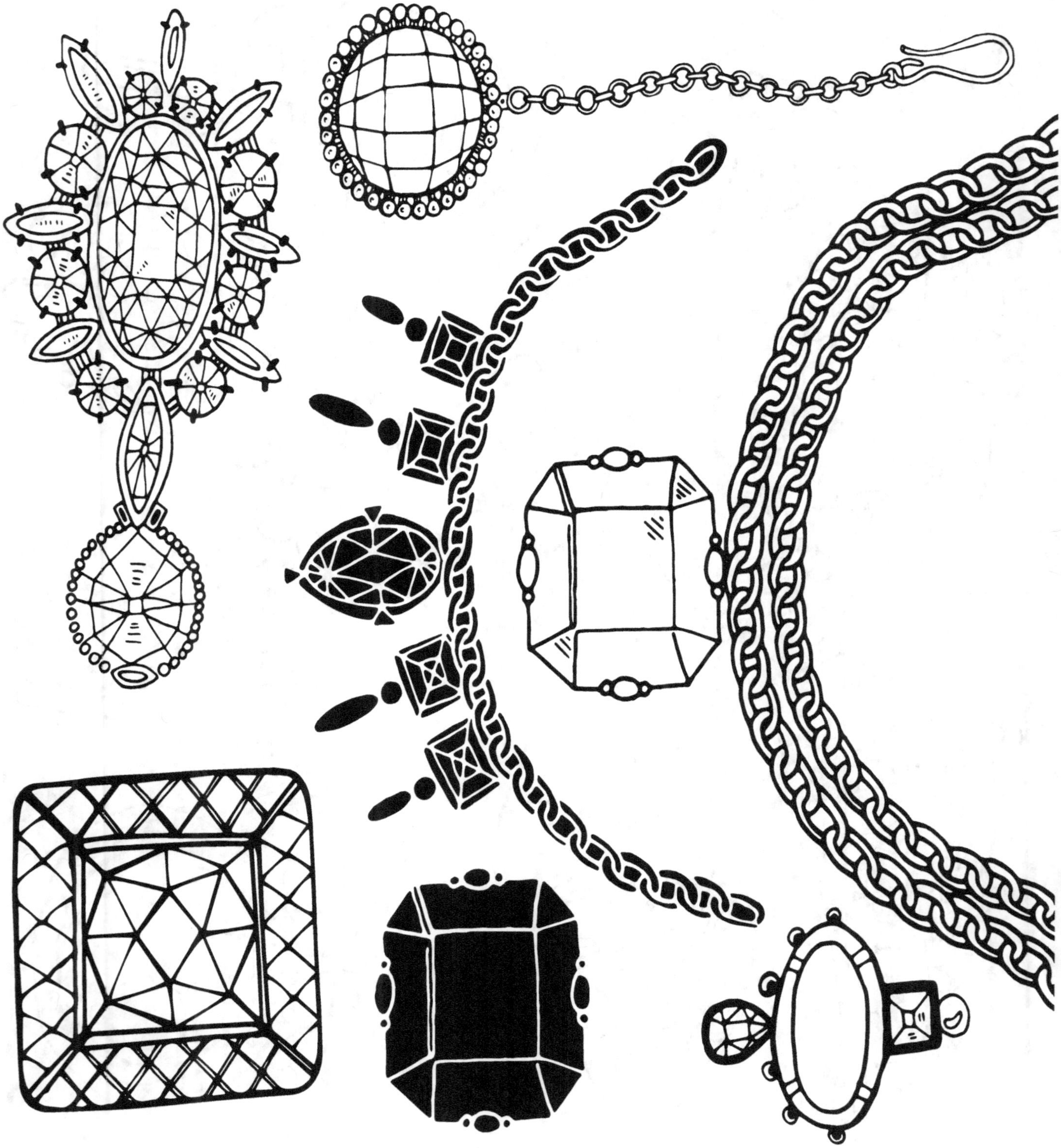

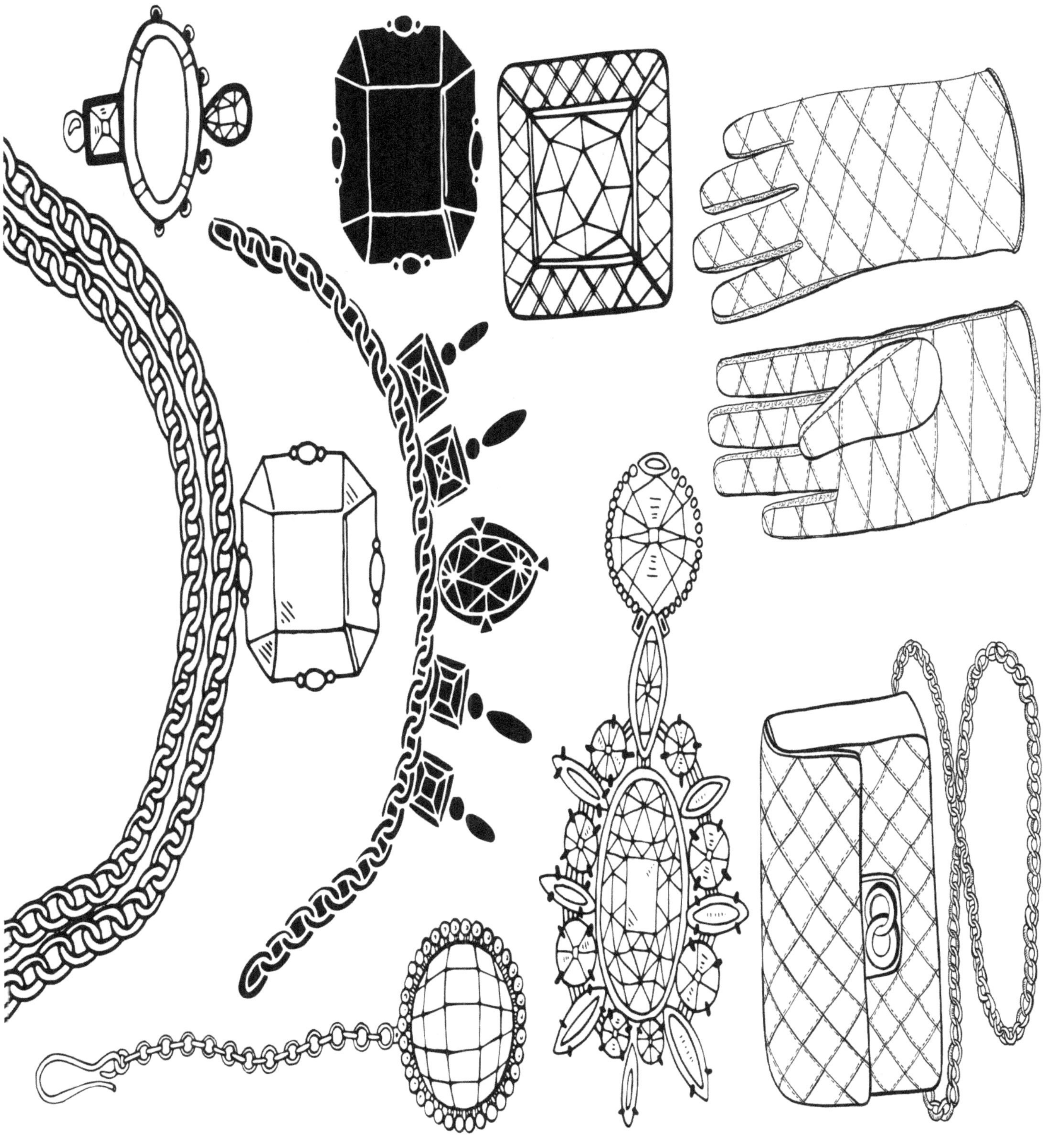

www.ingramcontent.com/pod-product-compliance
Lightning Source LLC
Chambersburg PA
CBHW081800280526
45789CB00008B/2936